ALONE WITH YOUR THOUGHTS

Aadhila Nowfil

BookLeaf Publishing

India | USA | UK

Presentation by *BookLeaf Publishing*
Web: www.bookleafpub.com
E-mail: info@bookleafpub.com

ISBN : 9789358739312
First edition 2021

I dedicate this book to Nowfil, Shiyama,
Haneen, Dhanish, Samirah & Masoud.
Thank you for being the catalyst for many
of these poems coming to life.

ACKNOWLEDGEMENT

To myself; Aadhila Nowfil, for pushing
through with perseverance in the face of
many obstacles. I'd like to think I am a
vastly superior writer than I was 20 poems
ago.

If I wasn't so narcissistic, to my readers. For
the ones who made it to the end.

PREFACE

As human beings, our brains are a canvas
for an array of thoughts. Most of which
brew and bubble, keeping our minds and
eyes wide awake at 3am.

This is a compilation of a number of topics
that have pinched my heart and ultimately
taken my mind hostage.

These poems are based on truth. Some
exaggeration, but largely truth.

Rant Against Racism

When you migrate to a foreign country you
immediately stand out

Confused at first, but as time goes on you
understand what it's all about

Your appearance, your dress code, your
accent, your food that's bold

It's unusual, it's different, it's hard for you
to conform

You observe your surroundings and finally
come to terms with the norm

So you brush it aside and the thought of
starting school keeps you keen

But little did you know that kids can be
really mean

From the first day you're branded an
outsider

Don't let it beat you, you must excel as a
survivor

The kids gang up, they harass and they
bully

They don't bother to get to know you nor
understand you fully

Your differences don't make you unique,
they make you an easy target

You don't belong, you don't fit in and they
don't let you forget

A tragedy somewhere, somehow labels your
whole community as being terrorists

It's clear we are not yet free of this type of
ideology from white supremacists

"Go back to your country!" a phrase that
continuously rings in your ear

At times, going out in public and wanting
to enjoy life just instils fear

These are not facts, they're mere opinions,
judgements, so let's just face it

This is not about freedom of speech, it's
simply about being racist

You know where you stand, making sure to
stay in your lane

But sometimes merely just existing with
differences can cause another much pain

You keep to yourself, minding your own
business, but that's not enough

"What are you looking at?" they'll howl,
even when you're not, now that's what you
call rough

You speak your native language, but to
some that's deemed unacceptable

"You're in Australia, speak English!" they
command, making you feel terrible

Prejudice, discrimination and antagonism

These are all words associated with racism

What gives them the right to hurt another human just for being different?

This hate, this attitude, this behaviour is purely belligerent

But don't let them win, don't let them steal your voice or take away your shine

Stand up for yourself, hold your head high and everything will be just fine

The beauty of life is that we all add something different, a different shade

You don't have to mock, ridicule, humiliate! Where's the love? Don't let it fade

Get to know us, educate yourself, there are so many beautiful cultures

Don't be hostile, don't ostracise, let's put an end to this torture

My Happy Place

The uncluttered scene wakes up under the morning light

Where sand meets sea and sea meets sky

The contrast of colours flourish; such a pleasing sight

With triumphant blue waves and caramel sand so dry

Copious grains fall through my toes with every tread

And the gentle breeze combs through my hair

My body feels light, thoughts clear in my head

As I take a deep breath and embrace the fresh air

My heart pulsates with the beat of crashing
waves

And the screeching of seagulls echoes
through my ears

The sea, its own master and we the slaves

A place now calm can quickly turn into
violent fears

The chilly water crashes up against my feet

Awaken by nature from a place of serenity

My favourite place, makes me feel complete

Leaving with tranquility is always a
guarantee

Dose of Darkness

It's like a crazy roller coaster, with the
highest of highs and lowest of lows

Finding the words to describe it, you just
don't know

Feeling frustrated, irritated, unappreciated,
agitated

Why is it happening to you? You just hate it

You find yourself in an unexpected
downward spiral, out of control

Affecting you from your head to your toes,
including your soul

You feel the weight of the world like a
burden on your shoulder

Deep in your sorrows, down in a black hole,
everything seems colder

No matter how hard you try, try to bring
yourself to be happy

Even the slightest of things has a way to
make you crappy

It's real, it exists, it has a way of taking
many lives

It's like a constant battle and a happy
ending hardly arrives

To the outside world you appear to have
everything, no reason to complain

But it's not about the materials, the
tangibles, the substantials

It's the peace within, the internal happiness
that you're struggling to attain

Your day goes on, you go to work, you do
your chores because there is no sick leave

No one can see your wound, your pain, your
agony, your perfect functioning self is what
others perceive

It is an ongoing internal struggle, some
days you win but most days you lose

And when you do lose, there are no battle
scars, no broken bones, not even a single
bruise

It's not just about having a bad day, being in
a bad mood, perhaps feeling a little low

It's a mood that doesn't disappear, a
darkness that doesn't fade, hopelessness
that doesn't go

Every now and then happiness will tease
you, but that crash that follows will just
destroy you

You have lost hope, you can't seem to cope
and all you do is mope

Life has become too hard, more problems
no solutions

It almost feels like this is some kind of
retribution

Someone help, help get you out of here, the
suffering is too much

It's real, it exists, it's a serious problem and
it should be treated as such

Go for a walk, listen to music, do yoga and
meditation they say

You've tried, you're trying, you'll continue
to try but it just won't go away

Every day that you get through, every day
that you surpass, you feel like a survivor

But you won't give up, you can't give up,
you'll continue to be a fighter

Dear Bully

A person's words have the power to make
or break you

What they say will all of a sudden become
true

They slowly begin to demotivate,
complicate, obliviate and simply hate

They criticise you for everything you do

It hurts so much you start to feel blue

Sometimes they pretend to be nice to make
you feel vulnerable

Then all of a sudden it hits you, their
harshness becomes unbearable

You're constantly told you can't do it

This will well and truly demolish your
spirit

Their torment affects you mentally,
physically, emotionally and spiritually

It seems impossible to escape the darkness
of this alley

Their presence towers over you making you
feel small

Their words cut you so deep it's like you
mean nothing at all

They have somehow managed to
manipulate you and obtain psychological
power

There's nowhere to go, nowhere to hide,
nowhere to feel safe and you eventually
cower

How did this happen? How were you
chosen to have this target on your back?

Constantly living in fear unaware as to
when will be the next attack

You start to feel powerless, gutless, helpless
and less is not more

You look around in desperation to find the
escape door

You're terrified to speak up in case it all
gets worse

It's almost like you will forever be stuck
with this curse

The harder you work the worse it gets and
everything you do is wrong

No matter how hard you try, what you say
or what you do there's no getting along

Destination Detour

The sound of sirens blaring

The sound of chatter slowly fading

So many eyes are starring

As I lay still, body aching

Today was our anniversary, a day of cheer

Instead with trepidation, you wait with fear

"He didn't make it," the dreaded words you
hear

Falling to your knees and wailing "don't
leave me my dear!"

The ground is so cold, please take me home

Don't leave me here, don't leave me all
alone

My new destination, a place unknown

"Beloved son, husband, father" reads my
headstone

I'm sorry I left you, it was my turn to go

I love you so much, I do hope you know

I'll watch from above and watch our boys
grow

And I'll be there in spirit when you're
feeling quite low

Dream On

Your mind is just a blank canvas

Till your head sinks in a pillow

Into a world of happiness

Or even one of great sorrow

Go where you want to go

Be who you want to be

Do what you want to do

See what you want to see

Creativity that comes naturally

Enchanted stories we create asleep

Adventures to escape reality

Etched in our memories forever we'll keep

Dreams are yours alone, you hold the key

Dreams are figments of stories untold

Dreams are meaningful so let's dream free

Dreams are powerful so let's dream bold

Part of my Heart

Meeting you was by chance

Befriending you was by choice

Instant bond at first glance

Best friends for life, let's rejoice

A balanced contrast like night and day

Polar opposites but interconnected

Common factors, limited I say

None other than you I would have selected

You lift my spirit when I'm down

And notice all the words unspoken

You know when lips smile but eyes frown

You know how to fix when I'm broken

We go on adventures far and wide

We share all secrets dark and deep

Life is blissful with you by my side

Blessed friendship forever I'll keep

Lost Amongst Words

Words create sentences and sentences stories

Immerse yourself in me, let go of your worries

Strap yourself in and together we will explore

The journey of strangers which was unknown before

Together we'll fall in love or solve a grisly murder

Together we'll become queen or catch a dreaded burglar

Together we'll travel to space or swim to the Earth's end

Together we'll discover treasure or make a new friend

We can travel far and wide from the
comfort of our home

We can visit the dead or go to a different
time zone

We can endure all the emotions from happy
to sad

We can always be who we want from good
to bad

The words on these pages better than
reality

At times those words can surely cause great
calamity

Tales of ambition, guilt or your
interpretation

At times filled with just words, at times
with illustration

Words can create fiction and some words
can create truth

Words can create an adult who had a
troubled youth

Pick me up and unfold the options that are
endless

Put yourself on a road to promote health
and wellness

Honoured

October 24th, the special day of your birth

The day your little fingers and toes graced this Earth

This marked the day that I attained my title

Having you in my life has been nothing but delightful

Such a tiny specimen, filling my heart's biggest void

Every moment of your existence I've watched and enjoyed

You've tumbled, you've crawled and now you're walking

You've gagged, you've gurgled and now you're talking

The feeling of coldness cured by your big hugs

Forever in my arms I'll keep you safe and snug

As sloppy as they are, your kisses are my favourite

All these moments together, indeed I will savour it

You're growing and developing and learning new things

I am thrilled and excited to see what the future brings

You're cute and you're crazy, you're smart and you're naughty

But I'll always be proud of being called your Aunty

Love that was Lost

The sparkle in your eyes gave me comfort

The truth in your words gave me hope

The warmth in your hugs gave me security

The passion in your kiss gave me strength

Your smile made even the stars look dull

Your eyes compel me to lose myself

Your hands as smooth as velvet to stroke

Your lips perhaps the finest of all

I suddenly started to notice the changes

I gave you my love, but we became
strangers

I gave up my friends, but you turned your
back

I gave you my time, but you were so slack

We drifted apart, my heart was broken

We didn't talk, the words left unspoken

We didn't hang out, I was empty and lonely

We became I, all but too slowly

I buried the pain deep inside me

Trusting the fact it's not meant to be

Building my bridge, I start to move on

And accepting the fact that now you are
gone

My Brothers, My Pillars

You provide guidance, motivation and
support; my mentor

You hang out with me and we have so much
fun; my companion

You look after me and keep me very safe;
my protector

You always have my back, even when I'm
wrong; my champion

Don't know how I hate and love you at the
same time

Best friends one minute, the biggest rivals
the next

No matter what's said and done I'm glad
you are mine

When things go downhill, you are the first
one I text

You say it how it is, even though it is hard

You've sacrificed your time, when I needed
it most

When I'm feeling vulnerable and lost you
stand guard

I feel so very blessed I just want to boast

You love me regardless of knowing all my
faults

You keep me grounded and reality in check

We've matured together into fine young
adults

Most times it's smooth sailing but at times
a shipwreck

The End

You're no more but your spirit lives on

My heart aches, I can't believe you're gone

Pain repeats at every break of dawn

It's been so long but I still do mourn

At times I can hear you and at times I can
see you

It's just my imagination, I know it's not
true

Without you by my side I don't want to
continue

But that's not at all an option and I must
pull through

I look back at the good times, that's all I
have

All the happy memories and all the love

The final dreaded moments a side I shove

And think about your spirit shining above

The role you played in my life, now left
vacant

They say that time heals, so I shall be
patient

Don't want to go on and become
complacent

There's no one like you, no other
replacement

I begin to accept that life will just keep

With or without you, the thought makes me
weep

Life goes full circle, emotionally deep

My time too shall come and forever I'll
sleep

38

Dear Younger Self

I wish you can read this letter

I wish I can tell you it'll get better

I wish I can comfort you when you've cried

I wish I can show you the other side

When you had no friends and ate lunch
alone

The taunts, the teasing, the phrases
unknown

I wish you knew that this too shall pass

Though it does seem, joy is at an impasse

Life is not about failures and success

It's about the learnings that we address

Yes, these lessons will be learnt the hard
way

But in your heart forever it will stay

If only you knew what is to come

How strong and ferocious you'll become

All the awesome people you will meet

All the traumas of life you shall beat

All those times you wanted to quit

You pulled through and to life you commit

Those times you wanted to disappear

Instead you faced it, showed no fear

There's only one way up from rock bottom

There's always a solution to your problem

Darling me, please keep soldiering on

The darkest of times will surely be gone

Expectation

Society has a calculation

Crack that norm with determination

Don't let that timeline break your spirit

It's your life, go on, just live it

They say, graduate by 22

That doesn't always have to be true

Job security by 24?

Who the hell made up that law?

Buy a house by 26

And throw marriage into the mix

Have a kid by 28

It all just depends on your fate

All the boxes ticked off by 30?

Life doesn't always have to be sturdy

What if I told you it's all an illusion?

We're living by our ancestors' conclusion

Don't be rushed by everyone else

Or hurried along by what society tells

Life doesn't have to end at 30

Life can even begin at 40

Just keep doing what's right for you

Live a little and have fun too

Yes, work hard but always work smart

Making decisions with your heart

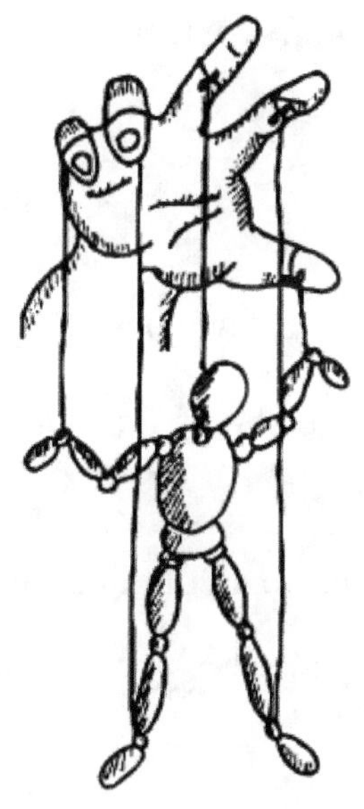

Self-Destruction

Feeling trapped and helpless

Feeling down and hopeless

Feeling cheap and worthless

Feeling stiff and lifeless

The pain of living, far worse than dying

No more tears to shed, you're done with crying

Soon you'll turn to alcohol and drugs

But all you need are kisses and hugs

The days stretch on, but the nights seem longer

To face death you're tough, but to endure life you're stronger

It's easy to give up but you're not a quitter

Physically healthy but mentally fitter

You end your pain but transfer it to others

This isn't the right answer because
everyone suffers

Mindless decisions in a moment of haste

Leave lasting effects of a bitter taste

You're given one life on this Earth

So just make the most of your birth

This journey is yours, you get one chance

Play, learn, grow, love, laugh, sing and
dance

Journey

The journey of life is like a journal

Some tales we share, some kept personal

These create stories, the ones that shape
you

To be the perfect image that others see true

The journey of life is an ongoing lesson

Some chapters are easy but some cause
tension

Those are the ones that will test your
character

You choose how it goes because you're the
director

The journey of life will leave scars behind

These scars tell tales of moments unkind

These scars that are invisible to the naked
eye

Share narratives of heartaches and moments
gone by

The journey of life is like a thousand-piece
puzzle

To put the pieces together you push, you
hustle

All these pieces scattered will never come
together

There's always a piece missing, you'll search
forever

The journey of life has no instruction
manual

You learn from mistakes and growth is
continual

You won't always know the answers to
"Why?"

Instinct speaks volume, follow it and you'll
get by

The journey of life is without a terminus

What's going to happen remains
anonymous

The final destination symbolises the end

Let's leave behind a legacy and away we
ascend

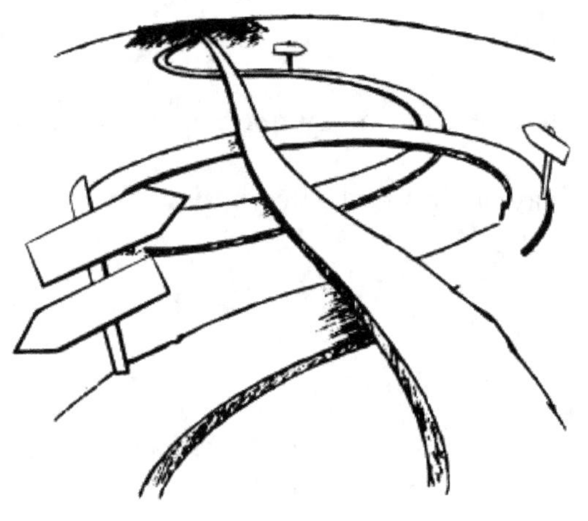

Strength

Mum;

You stayed up all night when I was sick

You know all the remedies that do the trick

You helped with my homework, though you
were tired

You're the only woman in this world, that
I've admired

Dad;

You taught me to be strong

You taught me right from wrong

When I doubted, you taught me to believe

You showed me the world when I was naive

Mum;

You've always been my emotional backbone

Patiently putting up with the tantrums I've
thrown

You're always forgiving, though I've hurt
you

The boundaries you've set, my success glue

Dad;

With you in my life I've felt secure

Your love and affection always pure

You always encourage to push a little
harder

To make life decisions that are smarter

My parents, my love, my parents, my pillars

Role models in my life, motivating figures

Without you by my side I'd be off course

Where I find the will to succeed, you're my source

55

Blessings

With the crescent moon I begin and I end

Throughout this special month, good blessings I send

I'm one of the five pillars of Islam

Remember to sacrifice and please stay calm

I teach discipline, control and empathy for others

Charity is essential, my dear sisters and brothers

I give you time to reflect and push you closer to God

Your worthy behaviour will earn abundance of reward

Each day before dawn, Muslims have their
first meal

Follow this with a prayer, now that's ideal

As the sun sets, we break our fast with a
date

The minutes are auspicious, please don't be
late

During this special month the Quran was
revealed

With this holy book in hand to God we've
kneeled

I urge you to read the holy Quran entirely

The stories it holds, will teach the way of
life surely

I'm not just a month of abstinence and
giving

I'm a constant reminder of our purpose for
living

I come once a year so make the most of it

Ramadan Kareem, to this month you'll
commit

Moments Captured

Snap away and capture that smile

And the magical moments in style

Snap away and capture nature

For on this Earth, there's nothing greater

Press my button and freeze time

To seize the minutes that are fine

Press my button for a lasting memory

I'm much more than an expensive accessory

Love lost and love found can all be recorded

Appreciation for this when your memory's
distorted

What you keep and delete is in your hands

Follow your heart and comply with its demands

Look back at times, at the path you've taken

Some friends, family and moments forsaken

A feeling of loss links into sadness

When looking back at childhood and all the madness

Feelings of embarrassment, love and nostalgia

Can all be evoked from a simple camera

Emotional memories will always remain

Some moments so deep, words can't explain

When your loved ones are no more

Look back at photos of times before

When your memory starts to fade

You'll thank me for the images I've made

Leave or Lose

It often begins with discovery and
passionate love

Being by your side is more than enough

A moment apart causing much pain

Holding hands tightly I try to remain

It's not long before the red flags appear

Where it went wrong, still unclear

It's hard to believe, one can change
completely

You start to abuse and treat me cheaply

My every move monitored, and trust is no
more

Where is the kind soul that I once knew
before?

My inbox and outbox observed daily

The trust is long lost, and you begin to
blame me

It now feels like a virtual prison

I begin to regret my initial decision

I'm feeling trapped in your grips

Nothing but lies rest on your lips

Your doubtful eyes are burning me

Just leave me alone, I want to be free

But I'm constantly being manipulated

And running back to a life full of hatred

The mental torture starts to consume me

If I leave, you'll find me, I just can't flee

You constantly say, without me there's no
life

But your actions contradict and state
otherwise

So I decide to stay and build what's broken

A chance willing to give as a love token

I want to believe that the love does exist

To fix this relationship with eagerness I
persist

Then things take a drastic turn for the
worse

Mental turns to physical, like a forbidden
curse

I've fallen into a predator's trap

Waiting for the opportunity to snap

Why did I make the decision to stay?

Why did I trust the image you portray?

As my body lays lifeless and soul departs

There's nothing that's left but broken
hearts